With transcriptions, lyric interludes, and thick description, Richard Greenfield speaks to, for, and about the dead, and in particular his father, lost to the larger orders of the kingdom of the gone. The poems in *Subterranean* sing through all of it reminding us that poetry has a vital role to play in the act of living and dying. It's gorgeous and heady work.

Peter Gizzi | *Archeophonics*

Like oracular and elegaic poets from Alice Notley to Itō Hiromi to Whitman, Richard Greenfield holds out to us a fistful of blooms at once lotusy and razory; his verses change the vision and cut the palm. *Subterranean* is a katabasis for the dispossessed, mourners and migrants who have not been granted a trip to Elysium but must instead tread and retread the American desert border: "giant yucca strained the ejecta / I had no tactic." This book reminds us that elegy does not help us reach a horizon line but, by obsessively mapping the distance to it, increases that unbreachable distance. The grief of *Subterranean*, then, is that it is ultimately terranean.

Joyelle McSweeney | *The Necropastoral: Poetry, Media, Occults*

One of the most enduring specters haunting American Letters for over 150 years has been Emily Dickinson. From her fiery lineage, poets as diverse as Lorine Niedecker, Fanny Howe, Rae Armantrout, and other intrepid inner rebels have kept the revolution of the continuous critique of prefabricated self-&-society going strong. And out of this feast of plucked flowers and winnowed seeds comes yet another scuffed up sensitive soul ready to not just "take flight" (in either a romantic or "avant" mode) but rather, foot-steady to burrow deep into the soil of materialist deliverance. Tending to the roots of our epoch, until the scowling winds of Vain Authority subside, Richard Greenfield (poet of uncommon touch, deft discrimination, fortitude, and tactical self evacuation) is carting over a barrel of wicked hooch for us tonight. Let's give this tome a real read, huh?

Rodrigo Toscano | *Explosion Rocks Springfield*

Subterranean

Text set in Century Gothic & Garamond 3 LT Std

Cover design by LM Rivera

Layout & design by Sharon Zetter

Cover photo by Aziz Archarki

Offset printed in the United States
by Edwards Brothers Malloy, Ann Arbor, Michigan
On 55# Glatfelter B18 Antique
Acid Free Archival Quality Recycled Paper

Library of Congress Cataloging-in-Publication Data

Names: Greenfield, Richard, 1969- author.
Title: Subterranean / Richard Greenfield.
Description: Oakland, California : Omnidawn Publishing, 2018.
Identifiers: LCCN 2017051239 | ISBN 9781632430502 (paperback :
    alk. paper)
Classification: LCC PS3607.R454 A6 2018 | DDC 811/.6--dc23
LC record available at https://lccn.loc.gov/2017051239

Published by Omnidawn Publishing, Oakland, California
www.omnidawn.com    (510) 237-5472    (800) 792-4957
10 9 8 7 6 5 4 3 2 1
ISBN: 978-1-63243-050-2

# SUBTERRANEAN

RICHARD GREENFIELD

OMNIDAWN PUBLISHING
OAKLAND, CALIFORNIA
2018

Also by RICHARD GREENFIELD:

*A Carnage in the Lovetrees*, University of California Press (2003)
*Tracer*, Omnidawn Publishing (2009)

# CONTENTS

Into the empire of the dead, of the
mole and the worm, the toil of the
tree inserts the powers of a strange
subterranean  will.  PAUL  VALÉRY

if one vanishes one stays
if one stays the other will or will not vanish

C.D. WRIGHT

# BORDER

Charon-crossing

Water vapor

Visping across

the silver surface

Ditty leached

from the error pit

Parent-death a

no-more


\*


Dear bright

ingot

every child-crosser

tastes it

on barrens

ceremoniously swabs

the body

with rags

filled with river


The dam holds back

Stench of the other side

    Through a chain link fence

    Flames

Necklaces of teeth

A yellowglow meal

Horchata in a plastic cup

    The roadrunner carcass

smeared by freight

traversing a prehistoric oceanbed


\*

I scour it sterile

Until I stay past

time should have

    and toll

Someone said

Bells

One forced to waif

The other to solid

Opposed

# SUBTERRANEAN

The mole noses into a hole and dements it     I see the dead in the
    molehole     he may be my hostage     unwilling guest hostile at
the doorway of the willing     I see the arm of the chair but not the
chair     I see only peripherally     the "effects" which make use of
light

One effect is a dull metal penknife     each blade's nail mark is an
    impressed-into smile for a fingertip     the small spey blade
    turned outward from its slotted bed     ends in a broken tip that
might fit into a screw's slot

    One effect is a wallet     black leather     a crinkly skin of
enwrapment     breathes through empty card slits     one effect is a
    bottle of cologne     I fingered the stench along my neck in the
mirror     *eau de black calf* standing on one leg     *eau de dry fly* in
a sill in a peaking crown of legs

Warm this week     middle happiness in walking a dog     I am
    alive and questions are more contrived under that condition
    the dog keeps lifting his leg to lean into the thing he would
    invisibly sign     an ending scrap of sunlight beneath a pecan tree
remnant of its orchard     it will be a memory of a scrap of light not
so much useful as available     whirling     the nutty debris of limbs
discarded ineffectually to the soil

    Animals in emaciated limbs anonymously look outward from
    the nether     mouthing their fading needs to each other because
    they have no discrete walls against which to reverberate their
private atrocities

Placeless grief revs in the queasy-sweet flowers in the obscuring
canopy     a net to catch the weightless junk falling from above
night     fully named     the huge tangled patriarchy of branches
the stars tingling     irretrievable


Comes an owl     vomiting pellets     birthing bones     an eidolon
among burned out stars that burn in the now     in a different
dimension     of dream-land laughter     there     again     at the
limits


Now I know nothing is unspeakable     or is contained


I swing toward the negative space of the outlines of homes
blue auras in windows     a marigold resonance in yards
the immaculate pretense the hostage wants     wreaths for
a welcome

—starved by a lacking lack—of light—
of water—of nerve—the rubber plant bends
into a hatred next to the deadfather whose
cilia pulse near—the deadfather retched
from the belly of dead fathers—the dry
canals of their penises—flood to feed the pecan orchards
—hear the dry snapping syncopation
of bat wings in the evening—these chaoses—
while my? hands the voids between my fingers
and the gaps between my teeth widen—
—the landscape is a false simplicity
of static surfaces—unknown sources—
urethrae gaping—numb testes—rectangular
pine box in which the deadfather is whole
and corporeal again—grape vines choking
fences—beneath power lines—nausea
from the transmission—
empty canals—service roads—
—infrastructures here
I cannot name—
the ceiling as the lifeless
underbelly—fields of chiles—my pecan tree
regaining after pruning—I have imagined
it as a ghost as the opaque whiteness of a
man beneath a sheet with the eye holes and
mouth hole cut out raggedly—but that is not
the other side—and when the apocalyptics
knock I will not answer and they will leave
their brochures—they want me to know this is the end—
that this is not somewhere you want to
resurrect—

# EDGE EFFECT

The delusions of silence     the dead clapping     dead little leaf-
clapping     seeping through insulated walls     a piece of hell in
this     droughtfreaked     arrays of limbs reaching into spring still
laden with marcescent     leaves     sun-cracked stonework
carcasses of fat moths under the porchlight     arid-mummified
belling train-crossing and no train     dog guts out     locked into
a nearby yard

smaller     the hum of the stereo amplifier     electric devices in
the bathroom recycle through charges     ducts fill with the pushed
filtered waft of central air     the entire cataleptic management of
environment that is the house     the network enshrouds the house
bolt the door at night     start exercise again     wait out an online
auction     yellow delivery truck and then doorbell     the doorbell
tones melancholic interruption

heated excess     thermostat high     ducts fill     the juniper drops
sharp seeds     wait for rain     rearrange storage in the crawlspace
await activation     expect dominion over slunkness     tomorrow
fear

money in the bank is a zero     to balance debt     file paperwork to
not have to see it     write new lists of old imperatives     chemic
air fumes from the outlet air freshener     loaded with floweresques
the ducts fill     these lacquered surfaces and their coasters
this pillow for the head     this head is heavy     this cat chews
the knuckle     this soft center is not a bloodbath
that would mean something in the vein

this rigor mortis hand is of a stranger      this graph forms
into a fainthearted outline of mountains      in the gathering of you
        within this measured macula on slow collapse      you
this speaking fog

# NONVIOLENT VIOLENT

I can fix it,
a book self-helpingly intrudes, here, after frost in the first week of
October kills the agaves.

Desiccated ragweed,
boxed into a vacant lot, veers in the wind.

No symbolic value.

Blackbirds combating above.

I cannot foresee
which one will drop from space,
be fed upon
    rot
or petrify on the roof.

Now it is not struggle—
It is tearing-to-slivers mating.

Hand-held camera, shaky:
a child riding its bike points to a pixilated emergency in the street.

Then a surgical score tracked over it.

There is no authority
in comparisons now.

Ninety-nine percent is a fact and also a metaphor.
*Is* is a necessary apparition of relation—
bloody copula.

Convert the scene.

Nature is not yet tamed. Nature is used.
In the critique of this, nature is also used.

Innovation is our heroism—
which is for money: wealth is heroic—heroism builds paper
utopias.

Many were happily atomized into derivatives in the hallucination
of
ownership. I want things I want ideal products I want.

Direct the corpse toward its next task.

It is evening now, the birds finished.

I don't know how it ended. I know birdtones, which I had thought
human, rose again in acacias.

Bass booms blocks away: a car with a scheme and a driver. Dust browns
the air between houses.

Now is the time for intimacy.

Sit down here, factually.

Let tongue blunder tongue into mouth—

I will be enflamed before myself
and I will be loved.

Crack my throat open
and scandalize me.

This 'authentic' pain bejewels my pied-gray hair. While I dye it younger,
the users of nature shall not stop.

There is
nothing to save for
for later.

## THE SECOND CIRCLE

Did not find the body     the body found me     the corpse will not listen
        though I speak more faintly to it     not reverently     than I
    otherwise would     though not an it     but a subject     killed by
    emphysema as reported to me     I was told the subject was alone
        on welfare     what other schemes could be forced into that
suitcase?     look at the wound trying to stand     look at the mouth
    chewing mechanically on its gristle     eyes sewn shut before the
    furnace     its narrow emperor form enshrouded enviers     I shall
    join you     have I opened eyes again?     walking paperwork
        death certificates     unsigned affidavit     after-belongings
    auctioned off to pay for cremation and packaging and shipping of
            ashes in a red sharps container     the joke     spoon
is as limited as fork     the subject's obese last lover wanted one of
    its suits     first it seemed a case of nostalgia     but then a breath
    later she scoffed she would sell it     because the subject owed her
        how much could it (the suit) get?     no generosity
        these violences wrestling the rest     I had seen the subject
    from the fuzzy vantage of the ceiling     had seen the dishes in the
    bathtub     scum on the commode     dirty towel hung from a hook
    beside the sink     burnt out light bulb     did they throw out the
        bed?     was it sunken in the middle?     art has preceded life
    this is the second time round the bend     I remember the whiteout
    pass     gusts scraping the divide when I brought him groceries
in a blizzard     in the Canto it is a buffeting wind     in the Film it is
a burning house     bright pyre for the fathers in the murk reflected
against the glass of the windows     of the sons

Did not find the body     the body found me


       look at the wound trying

                      eyes sewn shut
                          enviers

A noise,       tempest torn
      blast of Hell
      fury drives


the ruinous
          are heard,     lamentations,



when winter reigns
The starlings on their wings are borne



As cranes,


wailing, hurried on

—an old downed tree is a body holding
to a seeming—crimson debris in the split
rotten opening forfeited to the ground—I
have seen the backshades within summer
woods across a field—they visibly inhabit the
charges of atoms invisible in the shimmer
they stir—here is a company in beige light—
self-pity is two roads that split in a
yellowwood—
               sorry, traveler,
longstanding in the pause of a choice bent in
the thistle undergrowth, takes the other: the
better, grassy and wanting wear that in
               passing wears the same;
                              yet both equally lay,
and no step actually treads: I took Less

          —is the river flowing
     or is the river a long tub
          between dams—
          the answer is
     the appearance of him is an
     arrangement of him—and is
     of course transparent—

     the work of a shovel to get at
the 'day to day'—

# A SCATTERING THEORY

        I drove through the suicides     of insects rising
from pesticidal sloughs downstream of floodgates


Beer cans silvered in the grassy highway median below transmission
   towers in a fire-haze in August     wildernesses of incinerated
   pines


          The lord was not in the fire    He was ash


          Once he stood me upon his knee


     the Event dispensed into the sapwood of trees    a morbid marker
In the tree ring    The canes hewn from such wood?


                  He
     who coughed to death    breached into pillowy coffin


   he was not buried: no headstone no tangible no carcass no hole

By then I had hung the glued-back clock whose overt fatherhands
turned on a brass dais a fingerhut heirloom pressed particle board
and veneers in its hourly ascension and declension the hour chimed
one inch to the left too far wasn't ticking down:


The worst choice is to conflate his end with the cedar air of closets
where eating moths die


                                                    I rewound it
then I stopped it     the antique, already     by then I was treating it
   as my enemy     legless I knocked it from a wall     stared at the
   impermanence of it     twenty pieces     a friend tried glue     the
numbers separated into prick-points


It was not the end of cosmos
as he     this version of he     wanted it     as an elijah-wind


Not all forms exhaust                         Here lies a moan's ghoul

## EFFLUVIUM

My brother and I poured him from a red sharps container into the
short noisy river and the bonebits blinked in the current


The sunlight
illuminated the bottom with the pumice


He went
to the ocean
of the ocean


We waded through stranded brackish water as the tide went out


From the mouth of a cave I watched my brother watch his wife
and their son and daughter close to the waves


The little tide
eased into the estuary

## BODILY OF WATER

Scaffold    cerulean west    Venus risen    sole unstar    in the east
  the grand wash emptying into a reservoir cupped by a dam
its builders men with bathtub rings in their eyes


  Grounds    boaters building in hilarity a fire on the extrasolar shore
  stacking burnable material    this is not the entirety    descending
  the concrete boat ramp    knee ache    lapping rolls of surface
      feebly at the feet


  Heron    but I could be wrong    legs less-than signs on a rock
in the middle, fixed


  Threnody    that night not long after my father died when I saw a
man stepping behind the corner of my house— I didn't think it was
him as I approached him with a stone in my hand    no one there
it was a substitute—wrong ghost in the wild wrong


  The therapist friend called it normal—the arrival of the fact (after
      having not spoken to him for years) floating with the senseless
    pulsing crickets—or taking form in the redundant smiles between
telephone poles


 The third week I called the coroner—are you sure it was him?—
already cremated


  The neighbors' allnight motion-detection triggered by moths—
  yes, ignite    no, extinguish

It *made sense*—    a phrase    repulsive


   The unforeseen beach   the superjacent night sky by Vegas light,
   phased   the car stereo playing nothing good   but it's malleable
and neutral and requires less governance


   Everything said is crude   Is there anything left?   Any origin to
source?


   No one thinks of you   Him, or me?
   This is not even happening—   it's
   from the interim reconstructed
   This is supposed to help me   This is
   Not   It could   No, it will not

   But who's at the end of this convincing?
   I am

Happy     The knee is pleased

    The tiny fire sulfurous and shifting in the void     unseen beach
patches of human speech and laughter     out across the water


An iris is between them     between here and the old cliffs




       The critical heron is invisible then
       form less than action— that seems right—
       and able to imperson the partial

—after I repaired the car radiator the
coyotes cooed in the arroyo—though vicious—
not signs—instead mean sightlines between
organs— in transition I knew—less
than my cat spread on the cool floor
yawning—everyone I would want
near was unreachable while brides
and apocalyptics came to the door
uninvited—I would witness nothing—
my friend walked maniac miles at night
along irrigation canals— she carried
a metal mop handle and a can of mace
and a pink taser—she shined her
flashlight at a family of foxes who lived
in stockpiled culverts in a pipe supplier's
lot—eyes!—when she told me they were
foxes I said I did not think they could be
foxes—not there—not in the fenced-off—
I was wrong—once we shivered in a downpour
on the trail to the undammed river—filled
finally to the banks—close rows of cottonwoods
sheltering the lambs—my gums throbbed as
lightning strobed fuzzily behind shapeless
masses—that mop handle is a lightning rod
I said—I was unstalled—drenched—the cell
phone in my pocket quivered with messages
from unknowns fallen into unreturned
silences—lunatic mosquitos attacked—
obtuse evolution outsmarted the deet washed
from our skin—blood-welcomes—

# EYE SINK

Runoff fed the dead lake

From paycheck to paycheck the month was fortified with a balance
in the bank

Payday was the start of looting objects or objectives

Whatever emerged as an alert on the virtual calendar was brought
to sunlight out of the dust whorls     like all bromides

How much is in the tank, a friend asked

After the credit denial I am small in my shirt

A wing is stuck in the trachea of the worker's blower

This act of not-sinking is confessed through this comment box and
its request for comments

Play the fife lowly

Once I built a well: a thing, ocular at top, open, freestanding: flat
   rhyolite plinths a base for larger rounded granite stones, hauled
from the high desert, narrowing up to an uneven lip. At its center a
utility bucket and a little fisted electric pump—a cord tailing to an
outlet.


I adjusted. The volume, attuning to organic clatter, sounding true-
stream, faux primitive: the plastic precision of a whisper pump, as
the water lit over the rock: a noise, of pissing into an empty plastic
utility bucket.


I owned that pish bucket, and the draught from it was drinkable.

## BORDER AUTHORITY

All wrongs projected onto a landscape     scape derives from this

It is easier than one imagines     This is the surprise

Another century was more porous about crossings

Add this man landed in delirium in costume and get sick sublimity

A concrete marker memorializes the border   I was almost beside it
                a headstone of sorts

How tangible the exchange could be!

I operate within the rationale of peril

It's not as pitiable as it sounds when uttered aloud          Yes it is

This was the year of the census

They estimated the number of the species but ignored
            the conspiracies it took to survive where one should not

To conspire is to breathe concurrently

                    What happened next

I strolled the line considered in the binoculars of the border
            authority

I came to stygian place a lava field then the scorched grass
            of the playa

I carried gear a camera to expose the absconded light against
                the tracks of passed vermin who during the pivot star night
                slipped desperately into their watching holes

In my open eye I framed the dry domain

Blight and blight and adjusted the amplitude     Stopped

Shook sharp seeds out of my socks before I slid into the quality air
       of the car

Roughly fused into the excessive plain and the curve of the horizon

Obsidian sliced past             Giant yucca strained in the ejecta

          I had no tactic

# XERIC

Was a surprise    the locusts bloomed on the new year walk
    through the arroyo boscage in the scarified earth    mesquite
    and noxious thistle among the strew of granite    gypsum
alluvium    badland

    In the rain shadow    droughtful of all gist    try again

    A bird played still in the creosote growing from the albic earth

    What was the note of the bird then?    a dollar bird    its singing
staked in the wind

    We evictees from the idyll live in the gulf between sage
    and ironwood    profits forced into intervals    captures    contracts
foreclosings    even in this chaste exogamy with desert

    What if in the steps ahead in these several economies I could
    mortgage the month?    if I could make a lurching decision?
    to amend my upheaval?    to sign my filigreed signature?
    to refuse the endless payments to that abstraction *the balance*
which every year adds another principle?

—flower of the fan blowing the sweaty child—
abhorrent yellow streetlight shadowcasting
on a sleeper who sleeps in the machine hum
of vanes—fat little apneic thing—I should be
brained with the fan—four feet at the start
and three feet at the end—on the backdrop
mimosas burst into urinal pom-poms of chick
down plied onto boughs—unknown futures—
of perfect fluff—the palmery-plumery
dotage of lost spirits karmically upgraded
into better dotage—this is counter to the
twelve mourning doves nesting around my
deadfather extremes—loud losers who shall
not depart from a wiry tree of heaven—who
rested in the thin limbs and bent it down
and shat on the five-petaled flowers—nightnight
again—this was after Law—after Apostasy—
the moon arced the hills—the stench of tree
of heaven takes over—its suckers already trees in
their own rights—shut the door the streetlights
trigger on again and slab through blinds—
schizophrenia rises from the accumulating
leafy spilth from its brain—it is here
in the interstices of the tree of heaven—
in new year fireworks flung—in searchlights
crossing nonesuch stretches—

—earth
swallow this energy—turn it gold in the morning—
take the nightcrawler in my doorway away

# CEREUS

The spitstars fell
in the moonlight
roiled in on waves

hideous man-of-wars
inflated among the wastes
of completed things

~~soft collapse in blue~~
~~soft loss~~
the most

plain of birds updrafted
above the smacking beach

down here a headless seal
torso filled with ghost crabs

and nightblooming

the zipper opened

and out sprung

a sprig
of kelp

# CHEMTRAILS

What was that time like

    Preservation lay in self determination took life into my own paws

      I stocked canned goods in cupboards     practiced silence
        I was under the covers

     On the roof roared the rain storm cells bound the white instant
     down into the ancient animal-body slew of the earth    routines
filling the left-out drinking glass with violet hail the gutter churned
out milky fluids

        This was after a mistake but before a mistake

     During the alerts the neighbor unlawfully burned trash in his
      backyard    infinity smoke and samaras whirled down
and buried the door mat

I stood in line for a vaccine

## THE SMALL CUTS

The opossum may have been the lord of time

or a child reformed into this form      now I know the whiteness

made her female      in the window frame      pressing my fingers

to the glass      near her cheek and her tapered snout lined with a

bear-trap jaw of milk teeth      pink nose      leathery round ears

cat-faced with whiskers and rat-faced with black globule eyes

rat-tailed in naked prehensile rope      her five-fingered paws

clenched into potting soil

the hit

from left of the frame      the hand      its grip on the grip

of the haft      the back and belly and shoulder and throat of the

handle      the eye of the axe my sick recoil

where did he come from?

why was he here?

so many chops for her head to drop off      the mouth opening

and closing      the round open eye      though was she playing

dead or waiting for the bit to cut through her neck muscles

blood slung onto glass soaked into the bed of the boxflowers a sneer which was not a sneer     but the physiology of her mouth

my same limit decapped into chronicle     viscera     letting

a late hissing     after an askewed view     after the pouch-summer

inverted     moon hung up on still dusk white rhododendron

blooms whisping off gentle between lawn and flower box

we are wedged off in this pragmatism     what harm this creature

shall the axe exalt itself above he who chops with it     who

is the instrument of the hand     and who is the hand     he plucked

up the head by its ear and dropped it into a trash bag

took the rest by the tail     the bag     a givenness     cinched it


the last violence
to the small opossum
in the flower box
is creating it

—a wasp watching a third shaping a nest
beneath the swamp cooler vent—carrying
her ball-offerings of clay to the organ piping
between her front legs and forming it in place
around her eggs with her pressing head and
mandibles and slicking it with saliva and
humming—upside down umbrella—the mother
dauber hovers away and returns carrying
a tiny paralyzed spider which she places
into the tube and seals shut with her mouth—
the cooler hums—

                         the nest is a portal for
the deadfather—through its minuscule
bright tubules he larvally writhes and
enters—
         the drunk wants a drink—


the cat cannot help—she is split-eyed on
the shadows of junipers and flailing pigeons
playing on blinds and the milky seepage
of day onto tile floors while the refrigerator
hums—sap leaks from the wounds of the
hanging-on pecan tree—monsoon thunder
distant—
         my neighbors have stolen my
garden hose and watering can—

# RESERVOIR

The red core knows less than it should for clay

each day unspools a violent unpronounceable stutteringforth

　embrace marrow
bonecenter self stuck with its dividing cell
　disconnected from the pith


　the thrasher below the sky speaks the other of me
with unmoving thrasher has found me
　is abundantly burning
thrasher is duration unlike its salted other
　who sings from a heretic shapelessness


　fossilized tracks in the crusty layers millions of years layered
without human observation marked without construct of
　consequence　the tortoise track hardened in the mud can be a clod
in my hand rubbed softly into dust with my thumb　　diurnal
cycles in the blink of　none　　species here　　then gone


I go walking down a sandy wash
I was not here for the rainfall but I am here for the aftermath
　for the scour on the clifftops　joshua trees contort over the edge

　　　　　　　　　　　　　　　　　is it the edge?
　　　　　　　　　　　　　　　　language?

"     the amphiteater terraces downward to the pitted     "
"     ancient waterless riverbed widening into the recent     "
"     reservoir rainwater had become actionable it culled     "
"     from the whole erased days and traces to the west     "
"     glossy prefab houses metallic roofs     whispy puffs     "
"     barely clouds unmoving in the binary blue     "

what else to do with scenery—
with scene-language?


can't keep using it
cannot not use it


the speckled jackrabbits freeze ears     tuning     they come
in the evening to lick from the little pool from the drip system
their being

is not my scenery

the density of the tongue in the mouth
is greater than the volume of the cave of the mouth


get in the foreground with me


I'm a footprint from a hot foot in an unnatural shoe

# IMPERIUM

They washed their faces with camp ash and pressed charred wood
into princely teeth as I taught them whisker-scrape dirt beneath
nails pubic sweetness cock shift shrinking engorging navigator
reader of shadows sear fire closest to door smoke in the lungs
animal on the spit skins stretched out of the forest back into the
forest handle of axe the situated tools nickel and iron falling into
the foothills from the stars within without flint carved augural
staffs comets ingrained onto the eyes of my sons sparks chipped
into the tinder beneath driftwood on the beach salt rope fish oil
drizzle swallowing mammoths in the deep washing up kelp on the
wound the children abhorrently singing they were born without
women blackening the orphan points in the coals mollusk shells in
our pockets tackle storm throttling the conifer crowns the begging
ferocity-silence between the two sons caches of food stuffs the
alpha stoic thrift smoking the walls with sage hanging seed high
from vermin scattering the ash into glyphs vertical walls of pines
scored trunks conjecturing arrhythmic spinning stars visited by the
orphic herbal barriers to keep the fates out fog the drone of a
trillion insects were the admonishing moans of the unborn crying
for thrones thrumming in step I saw what my children would build
were crystalline shafts were dominioning eruptive by the flooding
channel done grasping my hand fingering broken glass from near
the river done with papa not a dream nor a nightmare nor a world
shared the perceived color of one thing simply bled over when
their incarnadine tongues became skin smashed bottles the vitreous
source thrown onto the wet mica dirt my watery children
demolished the earth they sang as humanly as possible

Growth used to be growth before it ate itself
but insecurity thrives in the indefinite the—
permanence is a kind of vanity a campfire
ring—older habitation—in the scrub the new
ruins of new frames for unfinished houses—
the human amplified—someone hallucinated
through the treated slats toward the murmuring
unfazed crickets whose reverie supersedes
again—the wind scissors through the toothpick
houses—striated clouds pass·over—no day
is named—plywood paneling bakes garages
gaping emptily, septic tanks unburied,
·     unpremeditated, backhoe toothmarks
in the dirt, unfinished rooms—
hammers stopped and the mating crickets in their
foothold are a dark-treble dying in the
grama—in the flattening of time replaced by
their progeny singing through my screens—
in this older suburban edging—
I am godlike in their timeline—though the
stridulating of their wings is older—
a gossamer intelligence triumph in the niche
among the rots of those who arrive then disappear—

# PANDO

A *red thought*

a heat yield

across tree rings

fire-delirium
  burned into

you who mean
    to continue
    who came here
        to drink
by the aspen
            clones

with elysium
expectations
        annually
        entered

yet it seems natural
        more harmonized

not
*to do*

*Most of the "luxuries*
                    *of life" are not*

to the aspen
elevation you
could have


    you hear
        when you hear
through our own ear

in winter
    frost
in summer
    quaking

    companion lives
simplified against
    the frittering details

or so it seemed
        these foils
could teach

*I spread*

an enterprise
without flowering
for ten thousand years

elastic with the sun

white trunks
growing through
own decay

a crude mass
simplicity is fires

scorched bare
the hillsides
to their edge

yet no simplicity
is barren

simplicity
is built

upon the soils of
disintegration

SEVEN WHISTLERS

Found a still thing
on the doorstep

a grey-winged moth

a golden plover

a stem
a leafy sucker
broken free of the trunk
from the pecan tree

three and one

moth was the spirit I mistrusted
            as the arrival
            of a letter

plover was the seventh whistler
missed by six whistlers
seven damned wraiths
drowned babies
or drowned sailors

who urged across the continent
in search of their sibling

I slept through the rain

its remnants in the morning
mirroring pools in the yard
the activated stink of wet earth
rose

from the hushed rigor to stay
and I lay on the threshold

Today we are burning the effigies and not the future. The entire system—the rock and the spore—fall at the same velocity. In isometry, two figures are congruent if one is transformed into the other by translation or rotation. We are scattered into the background become multiple and unincorporated and this is considered a crisis? This is a gift skeptical of looking up—it's downward into the detritus mud or communion with the unthinking unresponsive cell infused with history and limit trying to outlearn the blood—to gain autonomy lying to ourselves and saying we are reborn first while the natural trill in the spring celebratory reaffirms next. The sound of systems kicking on while we sleep the exchange markets moneying fluidly. This is evidence of one over infinity approaching and never reaching zero. It's easy to be certain of the front door and the cracked stepstones. Financials are forecast rhetoric linking the markets to weather because the markets began by trading crops. When apparitional tongues conduct through the wires it's not new news. It's the transaction's echo—the green sparrow radiant at the top of the telephone pole, intelligence gathering.

—received a letter but it was an ad for a big
sale—too broke—poverty is the excess of
lack but apples do fall to the ground—
no one is poor who has friends—

what was he wearing when he was found in
the morning—what if there is nothing for
him to have risen to—no divide—between
one thin slab of drywall and another—
between one shit and another—between
us—prone always—clawing into this
position—blended shadows in the
windfall—

ravens were eating a dead
animal in the road—such abundance—of
carcasses—abundant emptiness in the
stomach—as ravens tore—I couldn't
tell which parts they swallowed—carried
off—which organs they unpacked from its
abdomen—nothing so grotesque as an eye as
far as I could see—

the garbage was picked
up—some spillage—an empty can—label
said "cream corn"—a taste outside
language—

# THIS UNDERGLASS STRUCTURE

A black triangular bird glints behind the sun. A black balloon buds from a cloud, dropping sensors. The spookbox on the wet wall, centered in the gyre of the web like a remorseless listening ear, scans its keywords, its anonymous onyx leaking. Not god, not idiot savant. Box. Breathing an equation, it tings its cosmos until dozens of new leaves erupt from the black branches of a sidewalk tree, the antenna of this thing—the grounding of this thing—a flaring ant mound filled with meanness.

And where are you? Speaking for the box? You cannot help but be organic about it. Box and body seminally emerge onto the screen with the burden of disclosure. For the greater goodness.

This is the merge. The actual creation, a brief unclasped flower triggering, updating the quantitative self who shall sing and tell of its holdings to the box:

> what it assume
> it shall assume.

## MISUSE

The silver sling of water in sunlight

drinking fountain handle stuck on

The unemployed afternoon parkwalkers

are a guessed number in spite of recovery

efforts. Same value as a toe waging

a hole through a sock all day.

Same value as spitting the bloody

toothpaste into the sink. Same as

engine oil leaking. No longer what

one could call "drama" on the lenient couch.

The room was the hue of an exit,

of me, of a percentage of me,

of a percentage of the potential

of me. The windows looked out

so much more than me and I

form-pressed into the assuring

brown faux suede and the ambient

din of the wind soughed me into

the alpha rhythm, noncommittal

or, heedless, waiting for the news

to come on without turning it on.

Bodiless. Bloodless. Not touching

myself. Visiting myself, but speaking

the calculated lingo of the local

forecaster who wanted to offer a

view to the specifics of large

invisibilities, but then the larynx

vibrated as I breathed

into the historically-situated

moment, like an error

in the park, or a balloon loosed

into the cherry-cherry sunlight.

# THE FENCE

Sprung upon the mallow sky and aniline cirrus, the studded blades
punctuate the coiled steel concertina,

and none will slip over this spiraling rip nearly yet never organic in
its unfolding into this ribbon of cut,

      and none will grasp the shredders resting above
    the forty-five-degree angles of the top rail of four ragged
   barbed wires twined across the whitest portion of the noon,

    and none will leg over this tension stretched by wire arms
      on the pallid silk of the day the fence posts entombed
in posthole pools of concrete,

   and none will pass the chain-link the builders call the fabric.

  Whatever is secured is unseen, something obscured by the thick
    foliage of niche-hacks thriving between it and the fence.


them overthere

What slips over this whole of holes is the old red ash tree through the pied glaucous outward-and-over pinnate leak into the road's open plein-air, the will toward that sallow vacant space. Permeation into the half wings of the street lamps.

A young tree of heaven has found its route beneath the fence, its suckers emerging on the other side and growing into imitations of itself, unincarcerated. To clear the way, it has poisoned its competitors through excretion of a toxin.

Privet is at the chemical boundary of its neighbor, climbing the fence and using it as a trellis, pushing its buds through the gaps, its leaves laced unpalatable to insects.

Bull thistle is lengthening after emerging through the diamond holes of the fence, purple pincushion flowers scatter-shot with the turgescent flowers of green milkweed growing anodyne in a moist pocket along the concrete curb the builders call the root barrier.

them overhere

—found the deadfather's poem—the
left-to-me—flecked with black spots—
cross-outs—tongue displays from a pinched
pocket dictionary—and what the deadfather has
not yet learned he has been told to do—his
voice percusses with mine—in spite of my
defiance—that busted hicking rhyme—
—a form I wished unlike—
a turd in the nest—a childman drying on
a clothesline—a fraud—a saynothing
I read from the shoebox:

x

—and after this ersatz—let me add
the arc of the moon—the peeled bark
of a stripped branch handed into
a firepit—crow crowning on the roof—
sabbath in a mailbox—the dimcrested local
hills—star-spread without kinghood—the
candled want—balked at—the logic of a
cursed mouth—blowing out of it at
once—aboriginal and barefaced—
stillbirth of a canon—

I see children in a heap
in the park
                    amalgam
laughter
                    I should be
primed I should mark
a melody here
                    yet I deny
pleasure is here
                    I'm in
the mood for stark notation
to be ascetic      to blink
out saltpeter
                    I am
superstitious
                    the economy
protracts and consoling voices
unctuously confirm

cause and effect

crimped      pubescent vine
blooming on lattice

aquiver
            prostrate

and brambly      rapt

for accumulation

                    empty
six-pack holder
                    burning
trash

thunder without
clouds        scrim wind

the chimney leans wrong
the design is errant

many speak of assets
lost and found

sheared grass wet from a
sprinkle    flecked with
unreal dew
                      stars stratified
above and below
                      softness
punctured
                      I should sink
into a bruise
                      into mud

Let us fall        automatically fall
in value        fall in the auction that
is their empire

                      it is a risk worth
screwing        we must make out
the news which is advertising

their coffin your coffin        we
feel lately the daily lanes        we

drive within halt

    in the delicate
evening of emergency        we know

we won't know        how

to distinguish

from the sales pitch

we

would like to complete
a survey and receive a small

                percentage off

each answer is yes

on a scale
of one to ten

                        *sucker* is pronounced
    *succor*

                did the captivity choose

us or did we choose the captivity

how did we find the product

we ambulated    we
thought we could use this

so we
trusted this and were satisfied

# ALSO KNOWN AS

The stainless knives: treasured into the tillage after carving time, when August is between the dun bone and the planet. The barn held brown oily horses, fine-haired manes, flanks twitching, tails slapping off flies, muzzles in troughs. Straggler insects looped in the vapor above the corn tassels. This is transient conversion. The low creaking in a shimmery oak he might have climbed. Past no trespassing signs, laboring caricatures on the landscape—the farm now a private shooting range. Wooden cutouts of elk, deer, bear, propped in the pasture, their flat, painted facsimiles in a theater of guns. I am meant to follow king spirits. Say no more of these. Yet I am a king. Of null—as it should be—and these missives settle. On the ground, with a crowd of flies in clodded tracks. Pine-light slashes through to the understory along the strips of forest lining the pasture, brightening the stinging nettles and the small creek in the brambles, bubbling. White moths gyrate over the worm mustard, blanched-yellow along coarse bottom rocks. The narrow pods opened as beeports for the last of the bees of the year. These leaves roughish, these golden erections, catch in a sibilance: slender scarce short ascendings from the nearly sterile soil with stems of simple thickness obtusely toothed into the entirety— mustard or moths or a shed or an empty beer bottle or a whetstone or a piece of blue ribbon nailed to the barn wall, blue, and its frayed and bleached out F A I R. When the coroner asked for his middle name, I gave three: gangrene, jeering, and gene, aliases for the forms. I am a spray-violent cusser, for I have suspired his rarely feckless sentences. Of genes, I think strain. Or, stain. I cut my finger on the rusty nail and this viscous was also blood. Tetanus, maybe. Lockjaw. Spasms. Plunge the bleeding finger into a mound of fresh manure to fill it with new friends. Then I feel the backside of my face. The barn roof is two triangles that pay toward the sky. Lone cloud is a code, a blip on the vista. Shall we always be or shall we lay prone or shall we be both? Nothing will scare the cloud away. A drop, drop of the blood this afternoon with the mud dauber drone at the feet, the good innard stench on the earth now. My walk is a child. Walk the curving hillside road. Shell imprints exposed where the road cuts through the hillside—little things once wended into cambrian beaches.

Blown magnolias waft over the rise. White moths replace whatever goes for god.

  —the rose rose—wild and unwatered by
     the fence laced into the grapevine in the last
     light of dusk—fat hips unopened—the seedbed
     that never took was overtaken by ragweed
    until I raged at it with weed killer—why did I—
   the swell of cicadas and frogs began—
   I killed the porchlight to calm
   the flurry-bugs in the entryway—
    —Cygnus hung down—my
  pupils could extract the tail-end as the head
had severed into the floodplain of the dry river—
    —mistletoe fed on deprived
 leafless things that had once been lively hosts
  on the banks, sucked empty—[ ] was
  gone—
     I approached a dead animal on the roadside—
in the ultra moonlight I knew it was a flattened
raccoon—beside the bluewashed mailboxes
stuffed with papers and their nonlife offerings—they
  wanted to hold my hand—zero interest
  pushback through getting, spending, and
  wasting—this could help—in time the
  raccoon resumed with the macadam as an
  equal indiscernible—in the beginning
  my obstacle to swerve—in the beginning the
  downy tuft and the forty teeth exposed
  within their jawbones—and absence was
  more tactile in the the conglomerate tooth
  and rock materials of the road and the junk
  addressed to me the headless swan—

# SUN RAY

Listen.
Fanatical talkers, hectors trapped into rivulets of
sandstone, droning in a black scale fattened saints confused for
revelry.

But build a narrow satan of the voice here and parley. You cannot
hear the dead without believing them alive.

Dowser hangs over a water vein. Were you over the center-of-flow?
Bestow water, welldigger. Grow an orchard, homesteader. Smeared
stars circle above decades of stunted apples, wrinkled and burnished
in limbs.

Seconds open as windows. You refuse to hear the ticking. Time is
not a clock. It is degrading.

Protean clouds pump out of a coal-burning power plant
smokestack, vaguely extending a gray umbra over the playa and
into the alluvial foothills.

When are you?
Lips shedding off
the plain teetering
the axis stopping—

mute birds at last coolly chirruped, for the first time, for the last
time.

Your head decapitates from the neck for awhile
as it sips from a seap rock.

You shit below the anarchic splaying of meteors,
on the dry seabed of frail fishbones.

You wash yourself.

History scored on any medium by any historian is cutaway of
viscera.

*Jornada del muerto* is an intervening—in which the dying is only
dying and withers the cell-building on the path of conquistadores, the
errands of their helmets dropped along the wayside
and reabsorbed into the drifts of sugared stone over the milpais—sub-
sumed in piling, shifting, restlessness with a scree of fallen meteorites—
ascetic at sage edge, sage cupped to your nose,
said into the wind.

This exhaustive spacelessness immaterial unresolved shifty
blowing unsand

and you close your lips and eyes tightly to it to keep out the waste
of the bodies and their armors, these passersby—
momentary opening of the gaze onto horizon lines nowhere near
you

static in your gut matted
grains without adhesion into whole
darkness, darkness,
none in this magnification of sunlight
onto this one spot of the earth, terrifying in its diminishment
of whatever the self used to be. It breaks down
the old skin to new skin and flecks off
the pitiless semblance of you as your name.

The eyes grow roots
into the head for the first time.
There are the cottonwoods. And there is a spring.
A thriving. The base of a spring
emerging at ground level, at the level of the waste, at the level
of your tongue, at the level of every living being around you
with which you must share it.

Swing west, toward a cell tower.
Do you want to call someone?

                           Banished from others,
   but the spectral voice streams up from the basin to the peak and
    its antenna and striates and sieves through solid structures to arrive
in the spiral of the ear of anyone.

Yet still you are as alone as the namesake of the plain—
   when you wait your turn to talk at others
      though voice promises connection to the network of the living,
       where the sun ray is but a death ray in a garden, the type
       flowerfaces spread outward into.
       No guarantees, you must know.
       Xeric life, underfoot, knows.
        Their patch of shade is respite only for little things.

You, the macroform, cooked in the open in the shimmering auration of
pyrite flakes.

      This is a strict inventory of the moment of place in this
     moment so as to return later, in mind, to this edge effect—this
    overlap of the human apprehended as itself and the others it
   apprehended as their selves—incursions in which we will not reach
    any forms of uncorrupted, deified natures, self-exiled in the
  grandness of ego. The entirety of the anthropocene—the blip of it—
the mean cottonwood copse of us for now.

Assimilated to the backlands—to scarcity— we may live yet.

—into my field my dumb Venus rises bluely again
over the plain—the planet the only star allowed
though the incandescent gauze of the grid—and tender
and pink I am your gazer—the raw meat down
here—swing, bat—beaten blue in the sedge—I look
at you blue—what is that?—choking me for years an
ochre blue a veiny handblue—which proctored my
throat—unhelpful to the analyst—listen to yourself
snitch—were you even alive to this pain?—
we orphans of collateral damage are forthright in
thorns—and I will never have children—should I
tell you everything?—it is an inscrutable
moaning—an asthmatic speech I transcribe—
my answers consist of the grammar of
their questions—however eldritch or from the pit your
listening—translation is last rites—and hate has
slipped from the cell—and I put the brakes on—

# DONE

They say "tender" and tender

means "pay" I say tender

but mean "soft" they win

the paupers are planted into

the same sure ground but here

dead-grass plots are (un)

marked with hand-sized

grave markers and I am an obese self

children slide on a nearby slide

this lamentation rising from their

moth-mouths, this view from

the top of it, is ugly, concussive

trash dumped under oleanders

severed gate-angels reaching for

in the ditch a bearded man pissing

with inconsequential growls or

derelicts or transients, palsied

topias, the unutilized, the repressed—

buried there I anticipate what

wealth is made of as a man in debt

whose assets without feature

include an imported water-damaged

faux wood dresser made of wood

byproducts the ahistorical richlessness

of shopping in such aisles shall be

the scatter-matter of my own

byproduct, my estate and my

epitaph my unpaid debt

# FRIABLE

Slippage, in mindlessness.

Earthworms oscillating
in permanent night in loam and humus, skeletal-free, automatons
contracting in two-hearted motility.

All is conduit.
Thus, breathing
through skin and mediation of segments.

Everything unfolds

incrementally in a narrow now, in space, in a galaxy of perlite scatter,
within a descending nebula of roots and beneath a ceiling of rhizomes.

They are plugging holes
with surface debris—
leaves, petioles, flower-peduncles, decayed twigs of trees,
bits of paper, feathers, tufts of wool and horse-hairs—

and deeper, making a rich bed of castings everywhere upon which
are layered again sunlit surfaces.

We prefer the sweet air we confuse for the top, which we confuse
for the sun.

# DRUPELETS

Brief rain. The crackling percussion at top. The gutters run with the sadness of rain followed by the sadness at the stop of rain. The dry umbra beneath limbs. Vapor, faint in the warm aftermath. In the distance a peening bell, the school. Blackberries unpicked rot on the vine softening upon their terminals. This is as far as it goes: left on coiled brambles unfallen black stars in an unharvest. These black thumbs sink downward, liquefy, piecemeal into withered drupelets separating as a white gauze mold overtakes the shiny aubergine surfaces.

Drosophila larvae drink the yeasts of putrefaction. What might have been. The tongues that might have been seduced and ruptured upon. The plucked guitar note of green frogs rises as the dew point lowers.

A shrill raven sorrowcall from coalblack to inkblack at the margins of a river plain, delineating the ends of summer. They sound of satisfaction, full in their stomachs. Every day, more carrion. Every day, the somnambulant feathered stillness of daybirds, withdrawing.

Push it away: a woodfire smokiness in the air: moon in its waning gibbous: a continued release of elm leaves filling the terrain's recesses and dry rivulets beneath parent trees stuck into the side of the world: an incarnate shape of this point in the turn around an invisible sun: calm in the seat of the chair while lunar pigments hit the window in a transmission that pangs invisibly, if not inventedly, if not dreamily.

Pull into it—press face into the black mane of that head a scent of synthetic blackberry plenitude in the curves in the abdomen and pull it as a heap of down and rest the flaccid penis in the warm crack of the ass, and know the hours ahead by its past habits, the decision in the lymphs.

# POSTLAPSARIAN

My small fire
fractioned

out
in the firepit

in the backyard
a fence

around the impulse

Smoldering coals balanced

Mars in the sky
in an argyle
of stars

within the resting, vast
birdedge
of galaxy.

I submitted

to this astronomy
Beneath it

I crawled, as if
char were

a working
or natural vocabulary

Fire, preserve my luck

Open the abysses

the glassy starfield
and the gauzy

forms of desert
willows

and the lot
filled with ragweed

and new moon
the train passing

the graffiti on the cars

      scotopia

from the bonfire
shadows
skirted and tore
at a wall

it flared with portent
    of visitors

with licks and airy pall
    then retreated to ember

for distant
    things
close in the ash

# REALM ACCELERATOR

Terror-smidgens
or thought-shadows
or airy codas,
            the fruit flies—
     stirring from their rests
in the morning—
            swirl and level
up to the window light
until they are
     ornaments in the
spider's nightwork
shivering on bright-strings.

Time in the web
is the second half
            of life.

I peeled a Florida orange.
My thumbnail dug in
     against soft
     fruit, plying off
     skin and dropping peels.

I walked in cricket-throng.
One block I arrived
     at a taped-off crime
scene.
     A hit and run.

Police lights strobed buildings,
fire truck engine idled, the usual pieces.
Figures
            measuring distances
to a bodiless outline.

I stood with the bystanders

and their theories.


Weeks of flies flourished,
   fattening the spider,

kept around.

I floated—this.

Furniture arranged
toward a west window

yellows in the
   circular afternoon—
   wan, autumn.

How do small mouths chew?

{TRANSCRIPTION}

—what in the remains is undertaken—what
to covet—what would I die for—what stands
in for the totality—what form to take—where
to go—how to undermine asking—washing
dishes—in a handheld mirror the old acne
scars—in my forties I still have acne—
reading on the toilet—entering my life on
a calendar with reminders for the day or
hour of—this home I rent—I have rented
my provisional spaces with rent checks—
though each of these boxes was momentarily
mine—once when I was drunk I locked
myself out—forgot the spare key beneath the
doormat and slept in the car—my mother's
face phases every year—softer rounder
the eyes more recessed the hair wispier
the deepening splay of wrinkles—already
grieving her death—the unknown date of
it—how will I survive it—or the woman
sprawled in the bed asleep—we are loveless
and sexless and she hoards the sheets—the
debts keep me up—I barefoot into the
kitchen to drink water risen from a shallow
aquifer—the moon slivers in the kitchen
window—damn all sleepers—my cat I
buried in a birch box in the desert is out
there—I was stroking her back—she looked
ahead of her and not toward me—clear
urine emptied her bladder—and then she
was gone—my box collapsed inward under
the weight of shoveled dirt and what I had
used with naivety

# EDGE EFFECT

  This euphonious shrill climbing of human voices in the noonhour
this sepulchral withdrawal from them    then turning toward a mincing
opened-edge of them    wanting back in

Listen to it—the gross proliferating pile-up of us  funneled into the
ear canal and recast by the hammer and the anvil and the stirrup bones
and dropped into a deep room of the cochleal tubes and floated to play
aeolian hairs plugged into nerves:

        The noise of getting      rough semblances
        of those nearby

                *getting*

        —All of this is for you     the beginning of wonders
    the irruption into abundance collapsed into breakdown
          regeneration     that hope

      but one simply burns on another  all is fuel

      the other is fuel

—Of those dissatisfying equivalences to happiness
      sun is old     and emptied of significance
—Flowers hide behind the reserves of their verbs




So all beings rise   blindly   purposelessly   as the products
of innumerable opportunistic grabs single cells flooded by light in
the beginning    motile with a remorseless need to fuel    expel
and divide   labile




—What is different now?   one thing rises and another swallows it
as it rises and is engorged by yet another rising

Yes there are ceilings    yet none appear to be absolute

And stasis is no destiny, either

Exposed to a little morning sun until morning sun heightens
     into too much sun    it was always too much
put a trinket on   shake the peach free of fruit flies

Slice it open    gladness begins yellowy in the physics
of the stomach   the invention of the future tense

Yes it will rain
& nourish
         Will
grow        Will yield
  even the shuffling riot of the dandelions will turn
                into a field of white puffs and will rot
             and will be
                no less sublime below the belt
                yes sparrowsong
          dispersed and pulsing from one locus in the thicket

to another will be given shape or narrative
arranged into a First, Second, Third      yes
the ululation sings
for the gut




—Preen again

trust in causality

why not allow it? why simmer it to a set of values when it is

        a matter of time? a pang?

future earthlings will have their own

love is false if not carnal

        every morning the erection reduces to an automatic response

        grab it by the hilt      the privilege and burden of a metonym

        love was      put into something

        think of it separated from the vicinity of the beloved for a

        moment

        as a red essence loud in the roar of leaves in a

        wind storm as an unleafing because opening

        to another in a mutually edible state a wildness

        a wet sinking into the prehuman other a red field

a red aura

this braceleting the hand around its arm

and claiming it or this seducing unreality

leaves slicing sideways across the window frame

somehow closer to it from this position with this much

distance to it      not the creation

as in the gauzy green periphery of sparrowsense

it is one locus

among several

no new ground was possible until now

# NOTES

"Into the empire of the dead, of the mole and the worm, the toil of the tree inserts the powers of a strange subterranean will."—Paul Valéry, from *Dialogue of the Tree* (translated by William McCausland Stewart, in *Dialogues*, Princeton University Press, 1956).

"Bodily of Water": "An iris is between them" from Leslie Scalapino's *The Front Matter, Dead Souls* (Wesleyan University Press, 1996).

"Edge Effect" (II): "The beginning of wonders": *Cædmon's Hymn*; "Put a trinket on": Emily Dickinson, "The morns are meeker than they were —" #32.

"Subterranean": Edgar Allan Poe's "Dream-Land": "By a route obscure and lonely, / Haunted by ill angels only, / Where an Eidolon, named NIGHT, / On a black throne reigns upright."

"Friable": Charles Darwin's *The Formation of Vegetable Mould* (John Murray Edition, 1904): "Worms seize leaves and other objects, not only to serve as food, but for plugging up the mouths of their burrows; and this is one of their strongest instincts... Not only leaves, but petioles of many kinds, some flower peduncles, often decayed twigs of trees, bits of paper, feathers, tufts of wool and horse-hairs are dragged into their burrows for this purpose."

"Pando": Latin for "I spread." Pando is the name given by Michael Grant to a clonal colony of a single male quaking aspen (Populus tremuloides), a single living organism with one massive underground root system, discovered in 1968 by Burton V. Barnes in Utah. It is the world's most massive organism, weighing 6,600 tons. The root system is over 80,000 years old. The poem adapts language from Henry David Thoreau, *The Maine Woods, Journal,* and *Walden.*

"{Transcription}": "A pine cut down, a dead pine, is no more a pine than a dead human carcass is a man." Henry David Thoreau, *The Maine Woods*; "yellowwood / sorry, the traveler, longstanding in the pause of a choice bent in the thistle undergrowth, takes the other: the better, grassy and wanting wear that in passing wears the same yet both equally lay, and no step actually treads: I took Less": Robert Frost, "The Road Not Taken"; "four feet at the start and three feet at the end": Sophocles, *Oedipus Rex*; "The left-to-me" is the first line of a poem by Paul Celan, from the book *Lichtzwang* (*Lightduress*) (1970), translated by Pierre Joris, published by Green Integer (Kobenhavn and Los Angeles, 2005).

"A Scattering Theory": 1 *Kings* 19:11-12 (King James): "And, behold, the LORD passed by, and a great and strong wind rent the mountains, and brake in pieces the rocks before the LORD; but the LORD was not in the wind: and after the wind an earthquake; but the LORD was not in the earthquake: And after the earthquake a fire; but the LORD was not in the fire: and after the fire a still small voice."

"The Second Circle": includes an erasure of Canto V of *Inferno* from Dante's *The Divine Comedy*, trans. Rev. H.F. Cary, 1901.

"Seven Whistlers": An old English superstition said that seven birds, flying together by night and crying out, forebode disaster. Six whistlers was an indication that the disaster was in the making as the birds searched for the final member of their septet of doom. The birds were thought to be the spirits of drowned sailors or babies.

"This Underglass Structure": Title taken from Derrida, *Dissemination* (translated by Barbara Johnson, 1981). The poem imagines one of the switch boxes that made up the DCSNet (Digital Collection System Network), circa 2007. Steven Bellovin, a Columbia University computer science professor and surveillance scholar, referred to it, in a *Wired* magazine article, as a "comprehensive wiretap system that intercepts wire-line phones, cellular phones, SMS and push-to-talk systems." The poem additionally alludes to Walt Whitman's "Song of Myself."

"Xeric": "Each new year is a surprise to us. We find that we had virtually forgotten the note of each bird, and when we hear it again it is remembered like a dream, reminding us of a previous state of existence.": Henry David Thoreau, *Journal*, March 18, 1858.

# ACKNOWLEDGMENTS

Thanks to the Kimmel Harding Nelson Center for the Arts (Nebraska City, Nebraska) and the Atlantic Center for the Arts (New Smyrna, Florida), for writer's residencies, where several of these poems were drafted or edited.

Gratitude to Mary Jo Bang, Joshua Corey, Rusty Morrison, Julie Ezelle Patton, and Carmen Giménez Smith for reading the poems.

Gratitude to the editors and guest editors for publishing poems, frequently in a different form or with a different title, in the following publications: *American Letters & Commentary* (Catherine Kasper), *The Boston Review* (Andrew Rivkin), *Columbia Poetry Review* (Joshua Young), *Handsome* (Kristina Marie Darling), *Lana Turner: A Journal of Poetry and Opinion* (Cal Bedient), *The Volta* (Joshua Marie Wilkinson), *New American Writing* (Paul Hoover), *Phoebe* (Elizabeth Deanna Morris), *Pleiades* (Rusty Morrison), *Privacy Policy: The Anthology of Surveillance Poetics* (Andrew Rivkin), *Taos Journal of International Poetry & Art* (Cathy Strisik), *Thermos* (Jay Thomas), and *West Branch Wired* (Mary Jo Bang).

RICHARD GREENFIELD is the author of two previous books of poetry, *Tracer* (Omnidawn, 2009) and *A Carnage in the Lovetrees* (University of California Press, 2003), which was named a Book Sense Top University Press pick. His work has appeared in *Joyful Noise: An Anthology of American Spiritual Poetry* (Autumn House Press), *The Arcadia Project: North American Postmodern Pastoral* (Ahsahta Books), and most recently in *Privacy Policy: The Anthology of Surveillance Poetics* (Black Ocean). Richard Greenfield teaches at New Mexico State University and lives in El Paso, Texas.

*Subterranean*
by Richard Greenfield


Text set in Century Gothic and Garamond 3 LT

Cover design by LM Rivera

Layout & Design Sharon Zetter


Offset printed in the United States
by Edwards Brothers Malloy, Ann Arbor, Michigan
On 55# Glatfelter B18 Antique
Acid Free Archival Quality Recycled Paper


Publication of this book was made possible in part by gifts from:
The New Place Fund
The Clorox Company Foundation


Omnidawn Publishing
Oakland, California
2018
Rusty Morrison & Ken Keegan, senior editors & co-publishers
Trisha Peck, managing editor & program director
Gillian Olivia Blythe Hamel, senior poetry editor
Cassandra Smith, poetry editor & book designer
Sharon Zetter, poetry editor, book designer & development officer
Liza Flum, poetry editor
Avren Keating, poetry editor & fiction editor
Juliana Paslay, fiction editor
Gail Aronson, fiction editor
Tinia Montford, marketing assistant
Emily Alexander, marketing assistant
Terry A. Taplin, marketing assistant
Matthew Bowie, marketing assistant
SD Sumner, copyeditor